The Secret of the Rosary:

A Traditional Path for Spiritual Fitness

By

L. Voelker

Sodality Pathways

ISBN: ISBN-13: 978-1537493565
ISBN-10:1537493566

CONTENTS

Preface

Any form of prayer is useful for developing inner strength, calming fear and reducing pain. It can also be a doorway to another dimension.

The Rosary's power, tested and proven for centuries, allows you, whether you believe in God or not, to participate in a particularly beneficial discipline. It can help you to increase your spiritual potential, to expand your perceptions of the possible, and perhaps also to touch and accept the impossible.

This booklet hopes to answer questions about why and how you might pray the Rosary. By learning the "secrets" of this traditional system, you have the option of applying the energy of its practice in your life.

1. The Search for Meaning

The tangible, visible world of which we are a part offers no obvious explanation about why people exist; consequently, the universe can often seem harsh and indifferent.

Human beings, however, do look for meaning, and their search may lead to an investigation of traditional practices and doctrines that offer insights into the life.

Many people are exposed to Sunday school or to church services as children. Sometimes these experiences are positive and moving, and the person may stay with that initial faith. Some find that attending church once a week is all they need to give them meaning.

Others find that attending services or being part of a congregation is not enough. Often contacts with formal religion are negative. People can disagree with or outgrow the points of view expressed by individual pastors, rabbis or teachers. They may

L. Voelker

experiment, attend different churches, perhaps read the Bible or the Book of Mormon or the Koran in an attempt to understand the foundation of worship.

Some are attracted to cults and to charismatic leaders. Some find satisfaction in helping others. In the latter part of the 20th century, practices such as meditation became popular in the United States. Some people found the kind of answer they were looking for in techniques such as the "relaxation response" popularized in the 1970s. Studies have shown that such techniques can be effective for lowering blood pressure, achieving a state of deep rest and peace of mind. Done regularly, all kinds of meditative practices have been shown to have a profound effect on the mind and body.

And some people are simply curious about the idea of an outlook that includes a spiritual dimension.

6

2. The Search for Spiritual Encounter

Some people find meaning in a spiritual encounter, a personal spiritual experience. This encounter involves making contact with, and then receiving grace or inspiration or comfort from a source or power that is apparently outside of the self. This experience provides personal proof and it often is the groundwork for faith.

Spiritual encounter is often nontransferable. That is to say, it can be described and explained to others, but words usually are not sufficient for complete communication. Or people may understand a little about what is being said about the encounter, and they may relate it to some personal experience they have had, but they do not relate completely because they have not had a similar experience themselves - or they have had one but it is no longer relevant in their lives.

Many of those who are "born again" and feel that they have a relationship with Jesus Christ seem to have found the kind of encounter critical for their religious faith. Other people find their encounters in the mainline religions in which they have been brought up, others in relationships with nature or with lovers, friends and relatives. However it occurs, and no matter what its individual cause and effect, spiritual encounter can provide deep, lasting satisfaction and happiness to those who experience it.

The term "born again" can have implications that are useful in dealing with many different types of spiritual encounter. One of the most important aspects of such encounter is the fact that it can radically change the person who experiences it.

This kind of transforming encounter can lead to a living, practical outlook that seeks growth in a relationship with the forces that have been discovered through it. Whether one has his or her rebirth through a charismatic church or through reading the Bible, or through some other totally different event, the results can be similar: a profoundly significant personal relationship with a force or forces the existence of which is not able to be demonstrated by use of the five senses, and which is often difficult to share completely with other people.

3. What is Prayer?

When the search for spiritual encounter takes the form of words or distinct feelings, it can be said to be making use of what many people call prayer.

Although prayer can have as many forms as there are persons who pray, it might be broadly defined as the expression of a need or longing which is addressed to a force outside of oneself, or, perhaps, to a force that lives inside the self. Prayer can simply be openness to such a force.

The prayer might be anything from a vague wish or a silent request or hope to a long, formal litany, but its purpose is often to receive something that cannot be obtained from other people or something we cannot find the answers to in books or in training.

Prayer often deals with the impossible. Easy, possible things, things within our control, are not typically the kinds of things that cause us to pray. Possible things lie within those parts of the visible, touchable world that we understand best and can influence by our own actions. We can do the possible.

But when our needs or desires go beyond what we can control, beyond the possible, we often look for some outside assistance and guidance. We begin a search for some other power. We may ask the help of a God that we've heard about or learned about as a child. Whether with old formal prayers or with words that state exactly what we mean, we start to pray.

For a person who has found a spiritual encounter or for someone trying to find spiritual encounter, the practice of prayer can be a source of contact, of communication, interchange and of growth. Even those with a strong self-image and a firm network of friends and family often find the need for the kind of help that prayer can give. It is a help that, on the one hand, comes from inside of themselves, and one which may also seem to come from outside of them.

Those who pray daily may extend this kind of petition and conversation into a routine. A mother, for example, keeping the safety of her children always on her mind, may verbally ask for protection for them many times during a day. In addition to an occasional thought or silent request to God, some people make use of prayer beads to help them to concentrate on, enumerate, and meditate about their request.

4. What Can Prayer Do?

Prayer can be relaxing and reassuring. It can be a pause from the hectic pressures of life, a way of relief, sometimes an escape, and a visualization of things getting better.

Research of the past several decades has reinforced traditional religious teaching that repeated prayers have the same kind of effect that relaxation response techniques have. Studies cited in a number of modern books about prayer even provide a tentative scientific basis for believing that prayer can contribute to improved physical and mental health as well as to longevity.

Prayer can be considered a form of positive thinking that creates personal energy. On a very simple level, positive thinking is a way of admitting that we want something. The admission of that desire spurs us to action, and we either accomplish the task ourselves or put ourselves in a position in which that task can be accomplished through the help of someone else.

Prayer can also be thought of as a form of visualization. When a person makes a petition, he or she is not only wishing that something might happen, but also taking a kind of mental action to make it happen. Modern self-help psychology has popularized the concept that such visualization is pivotal to change in our lives. In this sense, it is quite reasonable that prayer would be useful.

Prayer can help reduce pain, stress, fear and anxiety. Asking for help often makes the person who asks feel better. Repeated, rhythmic prayer has the additional benefit of focusing the mind away from the source of discomfort and therefore actually alleviating a certain amount of the physical or emotional distress.

Another way to look at prayer is to consider that the psychic power of prayer may actually send out brain waves that may have an influence on other people or on events. While there is no way to prove that brain waves might protect another person from harm or warn them of danger, there is no proof that psychic power does not have some role in these things.

Prayer and intent seem to be closely allied. In studies concerning therapeutic touch and reiki, the *intent* to heal has been shown to be central to the effectiveness of those practices. It is not unlikely that the intent – need – desire – petition aspects of prayer could have something to do with its results.

Millions of people find prayer to be a way of talking to God, the saints, the Virgin Mary or a deceased relative or friend. People may also believe that these agents actually hear their requests and grant their prayers. In this sense, prayer is a way of reaching for spiritual encounter, an encounter that becomes a dialogue and exchange. Again, as with psychic phenomena, while there is no way to prove that prayers are always heard or answered in the way we might like by specific people or forces, there is likewise no proof that they are not.

As to whether one should meditate or visualize or project positive energy or say personal prayers or recite traditional prayers is up to the individual. There is not only something to be said for each of these practices, there is much to be said for doing all of them. In fact, mental and spiritual exercises generally support one another; they also are a healthy complement to physical exercises.

5. Does Prayer Really Work?

The religious experiences of millions of people, documented through the world's major religions, offer ample testimony that prayer can be an important part of a rich spiritual life.

But does it really work to get what you want out of life? That probably depends on what you want.

If the things for which you pray are related to inner peace and strength, to understanding, and to spiritual encounter, there is strong evidence that prayer works extremely well.

On the other hand, most people have had mixed experiences if they pray for a certain kind of event to take place, or if they pray for a material object to come into their possession. For example, prayers that you will win the lottery do not seem to be answered very often.

Still, one of the most confusing things about religious experience in general is that it does not seem to follow a logical set of rules. The workings of prayer are not the same as the workings of will power, or of the actions which one might take in order to achieve success in business. Good people may seem to have their prayers go unanswered, and those who appear to be less good may appear to get everything they want without prayer.

Whatever the real effect of prayer may be, it is possible that the effect may not exactly be the way it was requested or intended. When you enter the realm of the spiritual, you seem to enter a totally different dimension in which divine or psychic rules may appear quite different from humanistic or materialistic ones.

And how can tragic events such as plane crashes, torture, and civil wars be explained if there is a good God who answers prayers?

This is the basic problem of evil, the best answer to which is perhaps an acceptance that our existence is a journey toward personal perfection and understanding – a journey that is ultimately completed through service to others rather than through individual gratification or satisfaction or children or fulfillment or fame or material gain or even happiness.

In this context, apparent evils and losses, while tragic and bitter, need not take us from our path of becoming better or more complete, but rather help us to become more compassionate individuals, more capable of heroism, and unselfishness, and to serve as examples for others.

6. What if I don't believe in God?

People in deep pain or anxiety - for example, those who are frightened during an extremely turbulent airplane ride - seem to have no trouble praying, even if they seriously doubt the existence of God when they are safely on the ground!

It's quite natural for humans to appeal to a higher order, especially when things are out of their control. When problems seem impossible, then solutions may break the bounds of the possible too. So if you feel like praying when you don't believe in God, then there may be some other force or need at work inside you, whether it be what people call grace or simply a need to try a less rational or less linear approach to your predicament.

While prayer can have very natural benefits (like the benefits from positive thinking and visualization), its most dramatic benefits may be in moving things that seem illogical or hopeless into a spiritual or psychic realm in which miracles can happen.

7. The Use of Prayer Beads

The repetition of the same words, phrases or prayers is part of many metaphysical and religious systems. Devices for counting are sometimes used to organize and keep track of these repetitions. Prayer counters – beads made of seeds, stone, wood, clay, or glass, and attached to cord or wire – have a history as ancient as any of the world's religions.

Archeological evidence suggests that prayer beads may have been in use by the Assyrian peoples of the Middle East and by the Hindus of India more than three thousand years ago.

When Buddhism began in India during the 6th century B.C., it adopted the Hindu practice of organizing its devotions with a string of beads. The Buddhist recitation of prayers around a typical sequence of 108 beads is still common today.

Islam, which was founded in the seventh century A.D., developed prayer counters with

99 beads for reciting the 99 names of Allah plus a 100th bead called the leader or Imam. The Islamic counter is also used for counting repetitions of short prayers. By the ninth century, this prayer counter was a common part of the Islamic daily religious routine.

8. Christian Prayer Beads

Early Christian hermits who lived in the desert during the first centuries after Christ made extensive use of memorization and repetition in their prayer routines, and these practices foreshadowed the ritual of the modern Rosary.

The ascetic, Paul of Thebes, was said to have used a pile of stones to help him keep track of his repetitions. As he completed each prayer, he would move a stone from one pile to another. Other practices such as counting the notches on a stick were widespread during the first thousand years of Christianity.

By the 1100s, many Christians were keeping track of their prayers with beads. In early medieval England, the code of Saxon Law mentioned a "Paternoster cord" - a string of beads or knots on which to count the *pater nosters* - or *Our Fathers* that were said.

By this time, the early ritual of the Church included a Psalter - or the daily recitation of 150 psalms from the Old Testament of the Bible. The repetition of 150 *Our Fathers* was gradually introduced so that the common people - who did not have access to the psalms - could take part in a similar kind of lengthy prayer routine. And in order to keep track of such a great number of *pater nosters*, they began to use a *paternoster cord*.

9. The Rosary Tradition in Christianity

With the increase in devotion to Mary, the mother of Jesus, during the 13th century, a Marian Psalter developed that provided people the alternative of saying the *Hail Mary* prayer instead of the *Our Father*.

Also during this period, the rose and the rose garden became symbols for Mary and for the eternal life in Christ available through her intercession. The Marian Psalter was eventually associated with roses, and came to be known as the Rosary.

According to legend, the Rosary was further popularized by St. Dominic as a way of praying for the end of certain heresies that were spreading through Europe at that time. It is said that Dominic promoted this particular kind of prayer in obedience to a revelation received from the Blessed Virgin about the year 1206.

With the help of St. Dominic and his later followers, the tradition of saying the Rosary in its modern form became widespread throughout Europe during the next four hundred years.

10. What is the Christian Rosary?

The Rosary is a sequence of traditional prayers (usually *Hail Marys*) which has been used for hundreds of years to ask for help, to meditate on a certain idea or series of ideas, to open one's heart to possibility or grace, as well as to quiet fear, anxiety and pain.

Do you have to be a Catholic or a Christian to say the Rosary? Not at all. While the tradition of saying the Rosary came from the early Church and has been used by Christians for more than a thousand years, the Rosary is hardly the exclusive domain of Catholics or Christians.

In fact, there are reasons to believe that the prayers of the Rosary are meant to be used by anyone who wishes to say them. Modern tradition relating to the Virgin Mary and to the reputed apparitions of Mary encourages all peoples to use the Rosary for prayer.

11. Who is Mary?

The story of the young girl called Mary is a part of the Gospels of the New Testament and is familiar to those who know the traditions of Christmas. According to Biblical sources, Mary was chosen by God to be the mother of Jesus Christ - who embodies a divine plan of uniting all people with God.

Although the space devoted to Mary in the Gospels is not particularly great, Mary has become a dynamic element in Christian tradition in a number of ways, not the least of which is through apparitions. The messages that she gives us through her apparent personal and visible encounters with individual human beings can give us a more immediate sense of who Mary is, and they add considerably to the description of her character that appears in the Bible.

While messages recorded at her appearances cannot be proven scientifically to have come from the mother of Jesus - the complexity and quantity of apparition documents are considerable. And they provide a portrait of a benign person or force, a mother of humanity, who wants us to be happy, and who offers a simple but compelling system for reaching union with God.

That system - some of which is a part of the Virgin's recent messages at Medjugorje in the Balkans - involves the saying of the Rosary, moderate fasting on a regular basis, a concern for reconciliation and the cessation of hostilities among individuals, races, and nations.

12. Why Pray to Mary?

For almost two thousand years, evidence has accumulated that Mary, the mother of Jesus Christ (or a force not unlike her), cares about the world and its people, that she is an effective and loving intermediary between God and humanity, an advocate, in fact, in behalf of humanity, and that devotion to her does not go unrewarded.

There is a considerable body of testimony that Mary has been instrumental in numerous healings, and that she has brought comfort and guidance to those who have asked for her intercession with God.

This evidence can take the form of stories of a personal nature - people telling what happened to them after they prayed to Mary. Sometimes, however, there is physical, tangible evidence of faith and prayer, such as the thousands of abandoned crutches that can be found at the shrine of Lourdes in France.

While the information about Mary's role in human events is typically not sufficient to convince those who are not open to considering paranormal or supernatural kinds of experiences, it has been compelling for some who are familiar with the effects of prayer or who are willing to approach things which cannot be easily explained in scientific language.

Many people have found, after considerable investigation, that they believe many of seemingly miraculous incidents indeed should be attributed to Mary. Other people remain unconvinced or don't need to believe in apparitions in order to say the Rosary. The evidence in support of Mary's appearances and power is, however, sizable, and while its quantity does not necessarily lead one to faith, it does provide abundant food for thought.

13. Why Not Pray to God Instead of to Mary?

Of course, one can pray to God or anyone instead of to Mary; but many people accept that a person can also pray *through* Mary. The Catholic Church's *Mariology* (theories and teachings about Mary) places Mary within the stream of redemption itself, asserting that she is, in effect, a crucial part of Christ's plan and act of redemption.

Within that plan, as Christ has come to earth as an intermediary between God the Father and humanity, so also is Mary an intermediary - in a very physical and human sense - between Christ and humanity.

While many Christians feel that this positioning of Mary is inappropriate and has no foundation in the Bible, it is at least not inconsistent with the Bible to think of Mary as a personal, spiritual force who is our ally or friend in petitions to divine power.

Devotion to Mary is not, then, a form of worship of Mary, but just one of many ways to approach God. In this context, the Rosary is ultimately a prayer directed to God.

To those who are not religious, such "sectarian" matters may make little sense. In fact, the practice of the Rosary has less to do with theology and Mariology than with the desire to encounter and perhaps create meaning in life.

14. How Should I Start?

Since you are reading this booklet, it is likely that you are interested in or curious about seeing what could happen if you started to pray the Rosary.

A beginning can be as brief as a short inner request for help with some particular task or problem that you have, or even asking for the ability to pray. You might do this as often as you think of it, or just when the notion occurs to you.

Or you can set up a daily routine that includes quiet times of personal prayer and reflection. During such times the use of the Rosary provides an effective structure for setting a rhythm and time frame for your prayers.

You can purchase a Rosary or make one for yourself. Find a picture on Page 60.

15. How Should I Pray the Rosary?

Your prayers need not be formal ones and need not even make use of words, but many people have found that traditional prayers such as the *Hail Mary* or the *Memorare* are good ways to begin to ask for guidance or help.

Since the words of the traditional prayers come from the Europe of the Middle Ages, however, they may seem artificial or stilted to you, and you may want to "try them on" to see if you want to use them.

If they "fit," you may want to go ahead and use the traditional sequence of prayers for saying the Rosary.

If the religion-based language puts you off because it seems foreign or contrived to you, you may want to use petitions made up of your own words. Prayers of any kind can be a comforting and centering practice.

16. Why Repeat the Same Prayer When Saying the Rosary?

Repetition has been part of personal spiritual practice since ancient times, and it has recently been used in modern forms of meditation such as that popularized (and proven quite effective) in the 1970s by those promoting transcendental meditation.

While there may not be compelling logical reasons why a specific prayer request needs to be made more than once, there can be psychological as well as spiritual benefits in the practice of repetition.

The repetition of prayers or mantras (in meditation) can be relaxing and calming, helping to clear the mind and open it the possibilities of insight or grace.

Repeated prayers or words can also become a focal point around which to reflect or concentrate on a specific theme, need, purpose or person. If concentration wanders during repeated prayer, bring it gently back to the original focus when you become aware that your mind his drifted off track.

Repetition, as used in meditation practice, has been shown to have physiological effects such as the lowering of blood pressure; the use of prayer repetition has similar results. And, as stated before, repeated prayers can play a part in reducing emotional and physical discomfort.

The use of prayer beads, along with the prayers themselves, provides an extra focus, and, if you will, an additional distraction from pain or negative feelings.

17. Ways to Say the Rosary

You can use the Rosary in a number of ways:

Simply handling the beads of the Rosary one-by-one without saying any prayers at all - can be a way to direct nervous energy, allay fear, and open yourself to guidance.

The beads can also be used for repetitions of a personal affirmation such as "I will be strong," or "I am not afraid," or "I am capable of getting through this situation." Although there are a total of 59 beads on the traditional Rosary, you need not use all the beads, and there is no magical number of beads you need to use in order to get spiritual or mental benefits from using a Rosary.

The beads may be used as counters for repetition of a phrase such as "Mary, help me," or some request or wish like "Give me the strength to face my fears." The repetition of a short request or act of intent on each bead of the Rosary allows you not only to concentrate on your request and what it means to you, but to become receptive to ideas or different points of view that may come to you during your repetitions.

An improvised short Rosary of one-line requests can be said quickly and quietly anywhere - one prayer or one decade (that is, a group of ten prayers) at a time - in traffic, waiting in line, facing a difficult decision, attempting to calm down and gain perspective, or in any other situation in which you wish to reach out to find strength outside yourself - as well as to discover strength within yourself.

The traditional Rosary is said as follows (but remember that you need not say it this way in order to benefit from the practice):

--Introductory prayers (all prayers are given in Chapter 18):

Make the *Sign of the Cross*, and then say the *Apostles Creed* on the crucifix.

Say the *Our Father* on the first bead

Say a *Hail Mary* on each of the next three beads.

Say a *Glory Be* and an *Our Father* on the next bead.

Some people say the *Salve Regina* on the medal or link that joins the five decades with the shorter chain and crucifix.

--*Then continue around the rosary:*

Say a *Hail Mary* on each of the ten beads of the decade. Say a *Glory Be* and an *Our Father* on the bead between decades, and then continue as above through all five decades of the Rosary.

Between the *Glory Be* and the *Our Father* you may say the *Fatima Prayer* for universal salvation (a prayer said to be given to the children to whom Mary appeared in Fatima, Portugal in 1918): "Jesus, forgive us our sins, save us from the fire of hell, bring all souls to heaven, especially those most in need of your mercy."

At the end of the Rosary, close with a *Glory Be*.

You do not have to complete the whole Rosary or even any part of it at one time. And you can vary the way in which you recite it, saying just the *Hail Marys* if you choose.

On the other hand, you might wish to try a Rosary of fifteen decades - a meditation which can take between thirty and forty minutes - and which was popular in the Middle Ages.

The substitution of the *Memorare* instead of the *Hail Mary* in any of the various Rosary sequences can offer a different and powerful perspective on the long history of Mary's role in the events of the world, reminding us that no one who ever called on her was left unaided.

In addition to saying the Rosary while focusing on your personal intentions or on the rhythm and meaning of the words themselves, it is traditional to focus on certain events from the Christian New Testament. If you are Christian and wish to use these events as part of your Rosary, you may meditate on some or all of the following "mysteries" (as they are generally called):

The Joyful Mysteries:

1. The Annunciation of Mary, 2. The Visitation of Mary to St. Elisabeth, 3. The Birth of Jesus, 4. The Presentation of Jesus in the Temple, 5. The Finding of the Child Jesus in the Temple.

The Sorrowful Mysteries:

1. The Agony in the Garden, 2. The Scourging of Jesus, 3. The Crowning of Jesus with Thorns, 4. The Carrying of the Cross by Jesus to Mount Calvary, 5. The Crucifixion of Jesus.

The Glorious Mysteries:

1. The Resurrection of Jesus from the Dead, 2. The Ascension of Jesus into Heaven,

3. The Descent of the Holy Sprit upon the Apostles, 4. The Assumption of Mary into Heaven, 5. The Crowning of Mary in Heaven.

It used to be customary to say the Joyful Mysteries on Monday and Thursday and, during the Advent season (the four weeks prior to Christmas). The Sorrowful Mysteries were said on Tuesday and Friday and during Lent (the season of preparation for Easter). The Glorious Mysteries were said on Wednesday, Saturday, and Sunday.

If you are interested in these traditional meditation topics, you may want to read about the events of some or all of the mysteries in a New Testament and use the Rosary to reflect on their meaning.

On the other hand, if you are not Christian, or simply do not find it useful or helpful to concentrate on these subjects, then either allow the rhythm of the Rosary to select its own direction, or choose your own topics (such as a the safety of your children or the happiness of a friend) to focus on as you pray. In fact, each prayer of the Rosary could become a separate petition.

Rosary Novenas: A *Rosary Novena* is prayer sequence in which a person says the Rosary nine times, either on nine days in a row, or simply nine times over the course of one or more days. Traditionally, a *Novena* is said in petition or in thanksgiving for a favor, but it can also be a structure for reflection on a particular theme or person or phase, problem or issue in your life.

A 54-day Novena was initiated in 1884 at the Sanctuary of Our Lady of the Rosary of Pompeii, and it consists of saying the Rosary for 27 days requesting that some petition be granted, and then for another 27 days in thanks for a particular favor or condition.

It is not the numbers 9 or 27 or 54, however, which are important or "magical." More than a rigid numerical structure within which one prays, *Novenas* can be thought of as an extended period of reflection and concentration in your life.

18. Traditional Prayers to Use with the Rosary

The following are traditional prayers used in saying the Rosary. As you decide how you wish to use the Rosary in your prayer or meditation life, you may select some of all of these to incorporate into your practice. Of course, *you need choose none of them* in order to make the Rosary beneficial to you.

The Sign of the Cross

An ancient ritual of Christianity, the Sign of the Cross is made by taking the right or left hand and touching the forehead while saying *In the name of the Father...*

Then moving the hand down to the chest while saying *in the name of the Son,*

Then moving the hand over to the opposite shoulder while saying *in the name of the Holy...*

Then moving the hand back to the other

L. Voelker

shoulder while completing the above phrase with the word ...*Spirit.*

Although the Sign of the Cross is associated today with Catholics, there is no reason why anyone could not adopt it as a simple prayer that uses both mind and body and invokes three aspects of God: Creator, Redeemer, Spirit.

The Apostles' Creed

This creed is a relatively recent addition to the modern Rosary, and some do not consider it an authentic part of it. If you are not Christian, or if you simply wish to omit it, there is no special reason to include it in your prayers. If the creed contains a few statements in which you do not believe or which you do not understand, you may, of course, leave them out.

I believe in God, the Father Almighty, Creator of heaven and earth; and in Jesus Christ, His only Son, our Lord, who was conceived by the Holy Spirit, born of the

48

Virgin Mary, suffered under Pontius Pilate, was crucified, died and was buried. He descended into hell; the third day He arose again from the dead. He ascended into heaven, and sits at the right hand of God, the Father Almighty; from thence He shall come to judge the living and the dead. I believe in the Holy Spirit, the Holy Catholic Church**, the communion of saints, the forgiveness of sins, the resurrection of the body, and life everlasting. Amen.

(**Note: the words "Catholic Church" do not refer to the organization which uses that name, but make reference instead to a "universal (therefore 'catholic') church." In the broadest sense, this might be considered a community of people of good will who attempt to practice right action.)

The Hail Mary

The *Hail Mary* grew slowly throughout the Middle Ages from a simple greeting to Mary into the complete traditional form given below:

Hail, Mary, full of grace, the Lord is with thee. Blessed art thou among women, and blessed is the fruit of thy womb, Jesus.

Holy Mary, mother of God, pray for us sinners, now and at the hour of our death. Amen.

Note: This long version of the *Hail Mary* developed from a prayer of just a few words. Its history, therefore, supports a suggestion that a person might modify the current *Hail Mary* into whatever shorter form seemed most comfortable.

The Our Father

The *Our Father* is a traditional prayer taken from Christ's words in the New Testament.

Our Father, who art in Heaven, hallowed be thy name. Thy kingdom come, they will be done, on earth as it is in Heaven. Give us this day our daily bread, and forgive us our *trespasses as we forgive those who trespass against us, and lead us not into temptation, but deliver us from evil. ** Amen.*

**Some people add the following before the *Amen:*

For thine is the kingdom and the power and the glory, now and forever.

The Glory Be

This is another traditional prayer, which, like the *Sign of the Cross,* recognizes three aspects or persons of God:

Glory be to the Father, and to the Son, and to the Holy Spirit, as it was in the beginning, is now, and ever shall be, world without end. Amen.

The Memorare

One of the most beautiful and direct of prayers to the Virgin, the *Memorare* is also a reminder to us that no prayer goes unanswered. Although not part of the traditional Rosary, it might be substituted for the *Hail Mary* on one or more decades.

Remember, oh most gracious Virgin Mary, that never was it known that anyone who fled to your protection, implored your help, or sought your intercession was left unaided. Inspired by this confidence, I fly to you, my virgin Mother. To you I come, before you I stand: In your mercy hear and answer me. Amen.

Salve Regina (Hail Holy Queen)

Long part of Church ritual, the *Salve Regina* is still sung by monks just before they retire for the night. Like other classic prayers to the Virgin, it contains a greeting, an acknowledgment, and then a request for assistance.

Hail, holy queen, mother of mercy, our life, our sweetness and our hope: To you we pray, exiles from Eden, and we call to you from this valley of tears, in our conflict and our pain. Therefore, come quickly, Mary: Be our Advocate, and look upon us now with favor. Bring us home and lead us to perfection and our God, your son, O merciful and gentle, holy, sweet Virgin Mary.

The Litany of the Blessed Virgin

Litanies are some of the most basic and straightforward prayers in existence. In this litany of the Virgin, many of the ancient and traditional names for Mary are listed, followed by a request for help: "Pray for us."

While some of Mary's titles used in this litany may seem puzzling, each has a story and a purpose - the details of which go beyond the focus of this pamphlet. The lore of Mary fills volumes, and can serve as an interesting area of research or of casual reading. For the time being you may wish to omit names that have little meaning for you, or you may include them as part of your search for understanding. You might also use one or more of these short petitions in place of the *Hail Mary.*

The Litany

Lord, have mercy on us.
Christ, have mercy on us.
Lord, have mercy on us.
God the Father of heaven, have mercy on us.
God the Son, Redeemer of the world, have mercy on us.
God the Holy Sprit, have mercy on us.
Holy Trinity, one God, have mercy on us.

Holy Mary, pray for us.
Holy Mother of God, pray for us.
Holy Virgin of virgins, pray for us.
Mother of Christ, pray for us.
Mother of divine grace, pray for us.
Mother most pure, pray for us.
Mother most chaste, pray for us.

Mother inviolate, pray for us.
Mother undefiled, pray for us.
Mother most amiable, pray for us.
Mother most admirable, pray for us.
Mother of good counsel, pray for us.
Mother of our Creator, pray for us.
Mother of our Savior, pray for us.
Virgin most prudent, pray for us.
Virgin most venerable, pray for us.
Virgin most renowned, pray for us.
Virgin most powerful, pray for us.
Virgin most merciful, pray for us.
Virgin most faithful, pray for us.
Mirror of justice, pray for us.
Seat of wisdom, pray for us.
Cause of our joy, pray for us.
Spiritual vessel, pray for us.
Vessel of honor, pray for us.
Singular vessel of devotion, pray for us.
Mystical rose, pray for us.
Tower of David, pray for us.
Tower of ivory, pray for us.
House of gold, pray for us.

Ark of the covenant, pray for us.
Gate of heaven, pray for us.
Morning star, pray for us.
Health of the sick, pray for us.
Refuge of sinners, pray for us.
Comfort of the afflicted, pray for us.
Help of Christians, pray for us.
Queen of angels, pray for us.
Queen of patriarchs, pray for us.
Queen of prophets, pray for us.
Queen of apostles, pray for us.
Queen of martyrs, pray for us.
Queen of confessors, pray for us.
Queen of virgins, pray for us.
Queen of all saints, pray for us.
Queen conceived without original sin, pray
for us.
Queen of the most holy Rosary, pray for us.
Queen of peace, pray for us.

Lamb of God, who takes away the sins of the
world, spare us, O Lord.
Lamb of God, who takes away the sins of the

world, graciously hear us O Lord.
Lamb of God, who takes away the sins of the
world, have mercy on us.
Pray for us, O holy Mother of God, that we
may be made worthy of the promises of
Christ.

19. Spiritual Fitness: Beyond this booklet

The road of your own spirituality is an open road, full of unknown outcomes. In that life-long search, you may find that even a partial or occasional reciting of the Rosary in one form or another is helpful and calming. In moments of crisis, you may find the Rosary one of the most useful skills or practices that you possess. You may incorporate a Rosary or a small portion of it into your daily routine, developing a spiritual regimen and making it part of your life. You may find it a dependable source of reflection and growth and comfort.

If you are disappointed with your first recitations of the Rosary, if "nothing happens," don't be discouraged. Like any physical or mental practice, spiritual practice takes time in order for inner results to appear.

While miracles can and do happen to those who pray, they may not happen to you or the way you expect them to or when you would like them to.

No matter what your first experiences, however, try to keep up at least a brief daily prayer. Recited daily over months and years, the Rosary or a portion of it will keep you open to the kind of changes that can occur as a result of spiritual focus.

The effect of prayer, like the effect of a regular exercise and meditation practice, is cumulative. As with steady and faithful practice of any art, or the gentle but consistent pursuit of physical fitness, your insights and rewards will develop, and your inner life will gradually become richer. You will have found new allies, and a sense of connectedness, a sense of belonging in a different dimension, a meaning and encounter that you first started out to discover.

Finally, don't be discouraged or put off by religious language or by the word "prayer" and the way other people may use it. The acts of intent that you make in your search for meaning are yours alone, and you define yourself and your purpose by them.

Made in the USA
Columbia, SC
18 July 2018